# FIRST THOUSANDS
# THEN MILLIONS

By

**Jai A. Darden & Katrina Ferguson**

# FIRST THOUSANDS THEN MILLIONS

Copyright ©2016 FIG Publishing
www.FIGPublishing.com

All Rights Reserved. No part of this book may be reproduced, stored in a retrieval system or transmitted in any form or by any means, electronic, mechanical, photocopying, recording or otherwise, except for the inclusion of brief quotations in a review, without prior permission, in writing, from the publisher.

Unless otherwise noted, scripture quotations are taken from the *Holy Bible*, King James Version.

ISBN: 978-0-9828180-9-1

FIG Publishing
5834 North Kings Highway
Alexandria, Virginia 22303-4924
1.844.343.9829
www.FIGPublishing.com
info@FIGPublishing.com

# TABLE OF CONTENTS

**INTRODUCTION** ............................................................................. 7

**CHAPTER 1** ................................................................................... 19
**CHANGE YOUR THINKING TO CHANGE YOUR LIFE:**
  "Mental Preparation & Conditioning"

**CHAPTER 2** ................................................................................... 29
**HAVE A COACH:**
  "It's Easier to Get There with Someone Who Knows the Way"

**CHAPTER 3** ................................................................................... 39
**AFFIRMATIONS:** "Your Words Are Powerful"

**CHAPTER 4** ................................................................................... 55
**NOTATIONS:** "Have a Written Plan with Checkpoints"

**CHAPTER 5** ................................................................................... 75
**GENERATIONAL WEALTH CHOICES:** "Leaving a Legacy"

**CHAPTER 6** ................................................................................... 85
**EMBRACE THE PHILOSOPHY OF PAYING IT FORWARD:**
  "You Are Blessed to be a Blessing"

**CHAPTER 7** ................................................................................... 95
**MULTIPLE STREAMS OF INCOME FOR KINGDOM PURPOSES:**
  "Expand Your Territory"

**CHAPTER 8** ................................................................................. 101
**THOUSANDAIRE ACADEMY:** "Bringing it all Together"

**ABOUT THE AUTHORS** ............................................................... 109

# INTRODUCTION

Successful people plan, and they plan ahead. Do you have a plan for all of the major scenarios that could potentially impact you and your family? If you lost your job right now, would you be able to ensure that your family would be financially secure while you looked for a new job or other source of income? Are you losing sleep at night worrying about finances? Are you and your spouse arguing because you are out of agreement on financial issues? If you stayed on your current plan, are you confident that your retirement years would be ones of bliss? Whether or not your answers to the questions above are favorable, you need this book, **First Thousands Then Millions** and you need to join Project Thousandaire and the Thousandaire Academy movements.

If you've ever considered the need for a better financial plan, would you even know where to start? Do you know where to go to find all of the pertinent information, especially as it relates to your personal situation? Of course, you can find tons of information online, but it is difficult to weed through the volumes of content and determine what information is reliable and trustworthy. Also, there is no guarantee that what you find will be specific to your situation, nor will you be able to tell whether or not it represents a legitimate opportunity.

Well, the good news is that we have a solution and a SYSTEM. For our purposes, SYSTEM stands for: **S**ave **Y**ourself **S**ome **T**ime, **E**nergy and **M**oney. Simply put, it means that all of the research, the preparation and the assessments have been done for you. All you have to do is plug into this SYSTEM, apply what you learn and we guarantee that you will see results. (Note: You, the FTC and everybody else, will want us to clarify what we mean by "guarantee." We are saying that if you follow our proven system, there will be some progress made. We do not know you. We do not know your personal financial situation. However, we do know that the principles we are sharing in this book actually work and that they are proven techniques to improve your life. We do not know if you will read this book and forget about it—or do nothing at all. What we do know is that our teachings and our system both work and we put our confidence in that.)

Our goal for writing this book is to help as many people as possible gain the necessary knowledge to move from their current financial position into a position where they are achieving their financial goals. Basically, we want to help you move from Point A to Point B and beyond. In this book, we will share knowledge to assist you in overcoming your financial issues from the past, managing your present financial situation and preparing for financial increase in the future.

What we have found as we operate in our respective ministry, business, network marketing, coaching and consulting backgrounds is that many people are shooting for the financial moon and missing it; totally missing it. Missing it, like not even landing among the stars, just falling flat back to earth. Why? Because they are lacking some very basic and foundational principles that are needed to grow money. Not only that, often there is confusion around the processes surrounding money so that when they attend a wealth seminar, they grasp the "I am going to be a millionaire" message, yet are crushed or disappointed when they realize they do not have enough money or access to enough resources to take the next step. Without making the commitment and doing the necessary work, they want to go straight from zero to millionaire status overnight. That is just not how it works. Other than extenuating circumstances, you will not go from barely paying the rent to millionaire status instantaneously. Even if you do, you will not be able manage, sustain and grow the money in a way that makes sense. We've all heard of the "overnight successes"—or failures—about people who come into money quickly and are unable to properly manage it and the challenges it creates.

On any given day, anywhere in the country, you can find people throwing good money after bad into a pipe dream—spending their cash on worthless games of chance or lottery tickets, hoping against hope that this will be their lucky day and this time they have the winning combination of numbers. Desperate to "get rich quick," they use superstitions, dreams, formulas, birthdates and favorite numbers to calculate or predict how a random drawing will turn out. On-the-scene television reporters scan the crowds and interview people in line to hear tales and visions about what they will do with the money, if, and when, they win. Without fail, individuals share fantasies of exotic travel and new home purchases. They insist that they would continue working and give money to family, friends and charitable causes. For most, they start and repeat this process with the best of intentions, but usually end up with nothing to show for their efforts, except for less money in the bank.

Interestingly enough, a 2016 article in Forbes magazine informed readers that approximately 70 percent of lottery winners are broke within 5 years. A third of lottery winners file bankruptcy, meaning their financial situation is worse than before they won. Additionally, many of them find themselves depressed, abusers of drugs and alcohol, divorced and estranged from family and friends.[1] Obviously, that plan is not working very well.

So, back to reality and a focus on building the fortune you desire. How are you going to be a millionaire when you do not even have a thousand dollars in the bank? How are you going to be a millionaire when you do not even understand how money works, or how credit and debt work, or how you are supposed to increase what you do *not* already have? It cannot be done... until you realize that you have to start doing some things differently. Let's begin with what you need to know about money. By the way, if you don't feel great

---

[1] "Why So Many Lottery Winners Go Broke," Fortune Magazine, January 15, 2016.

about your knowledge of money or financial literacy, you are definitely not alone. Check this out and evaluate your basic knowledge of key financial terms and concepts.

The S&P Ratings Services Global Financial Literacy Survey is one of the most extensive measurements of global financial literacy to date. The most recent 2014 survey was based on interviews with more than 150,000 adults across 148 countries. Of the 148 countries targeted for data collection in 2014, a total of 144 countries successfully collected data and met Gallup quality standards, providing data to complete the study.

In the S&P Global FinLit Survey, the literacy questions that measure the four fundamental concepts for financial decision-making—basic numeracy, interest compounding, inflation, and risk diversification—are as follows. (The correct answers are below in bold.)[2]

RISK DIVERSIFICATION Suppose you have some money. Is it safer to put your money into one business or investment, or to put your money into multiple businesses or investments?

INFLATION Suppose over the next 10 years the prices of the things you buy double. If your income also doubles, will you be able to buy less than you can buy today, the same as you can buy today, or more than you can buy today?

---

[2] "Financial Literacy Around the World: Insights from the Standard & Poor's Ratings Services Global Financial Literacy Survey," 2014.

NUMERACY (INTEREST) Suppose you need to borrow 100 US dollars. Which is the lower amount to pay back: 105 US dollars or 100 US dollars plus three percent?

COMPOUND INTEREST 1) Suppose you put money in the bank for two years and the bank agrees to add 15 percent per year to your account. Will the bank add more money to your account the second year than it did the first year, or will it add the same amount of money both years?

2) Suppose you had 100 US dollars in a savings account and the bank adds 10 percent per year to the account. How much money would you have in the account after five years if you did not remove any money from the account?

**Answers:**
**RISK DIVERSIFICATION** – multiple businesses or investments
**INFLATION** – the same
**NUMERACY (INTEREST)** – 100 US dollars plus three percent
**COMPOUND INTEREST** – 1) more and 2) more than 150 dollars

FINANCIAL LITERACY AROUND THE WORLD
   According to the study, a person is considered financially literate when he or she correctly answers at least three out of the four financial concepts described above. We choose this definition because the concepts are basic and this is what would correspond to a passing grade. Based on this definition,

33 percent of adults worldwide are financially literate. This means that around 3.5 billion adults globally, most of them in developing economies, lack an understanding of basic financial concepts. [3]

Back to the basics... How did you do on the quiz? If you do not understand these principles, or have the discipline to apply them to put $1,000 in the bank, and if you do not know how to save $10,000, how will it be possible to become a millionaire? Why do we think that suddenly, at the snap of our fingers, we will have the knowledge, know-how and ability to make a million dollars in the next twelve months? It is time to get real and to start working on a real plan that creates real results.

Ancient writings talk about the fact that we can take the little and make much out of it, but those same ancient writings also highlight the fact that often we need someone who can show us the way and help us set up a systematic approach to follow. That is where the idea for Project Thousandaire and the Thousandaire Academy originated. Project Thousandaire is about helping you earn, save and grow thousands, which ultimately can turn into millions for you, your family and your future. Thousandaire Academy is actually the educational institution whose goal is to help you to increase your finances.

---

[3] "Financial Literacy Around the World: Insights from the Standard & Poor's Ratings Services Global Financial Literacy Survey," 2014.

Imagine how your life could change if your finances increased ten-fold; meaning, if you have $1,000 in your wallet, $25,000 in savings and $75,000 in retirement that those numbers would increase to $10,000, $250,000 and $750,000 respectively. At that point, you and your family would be well on your way to millionaire status. First hundreds, then thousands, then millions – that is the process that we want to challenge you to embrace following the steps in this book.

This entire journey is really about having a road map. With a road map that tells you how to get somewhere, the trip becomes a lot simpler. If you are going on vacation to Disney World and do not know how to get there, you should consult a map or use GPS in the car or on your cell phone to point out the direction. With those step-by-step or play-by-play instructions and your willingness to follow them, most often you will get to your final destination. That is what this is all about, mapping out the journey and narrowing down the systemic steps that are needed to get you where you want to go.

## WHY SHOULD YOU LISTEN TO US?

**Jai A. Darden** has an extensive background in banking and finance, having worked for one of the largest financial institutions in the world. As a vice president for that company, Jai worked in their low-to-moderate income unit, as well as with some of the more affluent and wealthiest individuals in the world. All of those customers were a part of his portfolio, and he was responsible for more than $600 million in terms of operating the profit and loss (P&L) for that business unit.

While working with that company, Jai noticed the people who came in on a daily basis, whether they had tons of money or simply lived paycheck to paycheck, all had the same struggle. They just really wanted to know two basic things: how to move from one financial position to the next and how to take care of and grow the money that they already had. Jai was bothered because he saw that people wanted to know, but did not really know what to ask and who to trust. It was not that they were OK with being bad at finances, they simply didn't have a guide or plan—nor anyone to show them the way.

**Katrina Ferguson** is more the entrepreneurial type. Having been involved in the business and network marketing industries since high school, she attempted the corporate route and learned that when life happened, as it does, she found herself as a single parent, trying to keep food on the table and a roof over the heads of her three children. In short order, she returned to network marketing and was able to create a tremendous income, not just for herself, but for others as well.

Her challenge, like many others, was figuring out what to do once she made a significant amount of money. How do you increase it? How should you spend it? How should you not spend it? What is a real asset versus a real liability? Those were the kinds of questions she and others had, but did not have a reliable vehicle to get the answers the needed.

Currently, Jai and Katrina consult with network marketing companies, businesses, ministries and individuals to help them achieve their goals and live their purposes by systematically increasing their finances, thereby buying their time back from their employers and other activities, which are not in alignment with their life's purpose.

Working and serving together, Jai and Katrina have created millions of dollars of income for their families and for others. Collectively, they own several profitable businesses, allowing them to help others, give back to their communities and support many ministries around the world, more specifically in the United States and Africa. In Nakuru, for instance, the ability to simply buy a cow for an orphanage so that they can have milk for themselves and sell the rest to create an additional stream of revenue is a blessing. Because of our support—along with countless others—these children are able to learn how to better support themselves, sustain the village greenhouse and everything else that they need. Those are the things that are important to us... being able to help people. Money is a tool. We use money to live on purpose and to do destiny. In order to do those things, you have to understand how money works—and it helps to follow along with people who are already where you want to be.

Project Thousandaire and the Thousandaire Academy were designed to help churches, schools and nonprofits get a cursory understanding of the definition of wealth and how money works. We know that the key to accumulating wealth begins with making changes in your current situation. You do not have to figure out how to change your financial situation on your own. There are experts, counselors and financial planners within our network who have already done the research, learned the lessons and are ready to share their findings with you. It's easy to make the mistake of feeling like you have to use trial and error to find your way to your destiny. However, that is not the case. There is safety in a multitude of counselors, and we invite you to join us as we all work together to achieve more, so that we can do more and give more for Kingdom purposes.

# Chapter 1

# Change Your Thinking to Change Your Life:
## Mental Preparation & Conditioning

If you want to change your life, you must change the way you think about your life. You must realize that if your current thinking was going to make you wealthy, then you would already be wealthy. The life you live today is the sum total of the choices that you made yesterday. This is why we must choose wisely. Part of your involvement with Project Thousandaire and the Thousandaire Academy is our guidance as we begin the process of dissecting your thoughts and ideas around wealth and money, more specifically. What are you meditating on regularly? We need to take the unproductive thinking and replace it with productive thinking. These are the thoughts that the very wealthy are already thinking, and as a result, producing a life that they not only dreamed of, but also created with their thoughts.

You attract what you think about most. With that in mind, the only solution is to change your thinking and change your life. Best-selling author Dennis Kimbro, Ph.D. says that "wealth is not a function of circumstances; it is a function of decision and choice." And choice is a function of your thinking. If you are not focused on the way you think, that is an indication that you may not be living your life deliberately and on purpose. Maybe your life is even spinning out of control, kind of like your thoughts. What are you thinking about? What are the priorities in your life right now? On what topics do you invest your mental energy and focus? The way your mind works will dictate the way your life works.

Scientists have proven this fact over and over again in the production and development of pharmaceuticals and the corresponding studies. There will be a study, and researchers may take a group of unsuspecting subjects; some they give the real medicine and others they give a placebo. The interesting fact is that not only do the subjects that are taking the real medication begin to feel better, so do those taking the placebo. This is because the mind is so powerful that just the *thought* that the pill is medicine and working to cure their ailment is often enough for the brain to begin healing the ailment. The power of our minds is amazing!

*Live your life deliberately and on purpose.*

Part of changing your thinking is changing how you think about what you think about – which we will refer to as framing. Two people can take the same situation, frame (position, value and view) it differently and produce totally different outcomes emotionally and physically. For instance, we have been taught to "cut back" on our spending; to buy no-frills and generic brands of this and that. We would like to submit a different thought to you. Even though for a period of time you may have to buy the item that costs less, do not allow that to become part of your thinking. As a matter of fact, rather than focusing on spending less, focus on making more money. Remember, what you focus on expands, positive or negative. So if you focus on cutting back on your expenses, you will cause more cut-backs to come. If you focus on the dream house and the dream cars, on being able to live and give at whatever levels you choose, you will begin to see more ideas. As you act on them, more money comes in your direction. Have an "increase mindset" and only think on, focus on, meditate on those things that will bring you more of what you want.

Earlier, we talked about lottery winners. In terms of framing, how do you think about the lottery? Some say, "if only I could win," while others say, "why would I waste the money to play?" Even more, some think that if somebody simply gave them money, like winning the lottery or being left a large inheritance or some other kind of handout, then they could find their way to financial success. They are looking for a handout. Let us be the first to tell you, if you did not already know. The only "hand-out" you need is at the end of your sleeve.

Do not misunderstand, we are not saying that from time to time we do not need a *hand-up* when we find ourselves in a position where we need some additional help. Social services and the programs that it offers are not inherently bad. It is the abuse of the programs and the effect of that abuse on our thinking that is a problem. Public assistance should not be a way of life. Should you find yourself in a position to use any kind of public assistance, purpose in your heart to use it the way it was designed, for a minimal amount of time. The damage that this extended dependence on these programs can do to your mindset and confidence can be extremely detrimental. It bears repeating, we are not saying that welfare is bad, just that when it becomes a way of life, it has negative effects on overall mental well-being. When you are given money and resources without having to work for them, it tends to negatively affect your self-esteem and confidence.

> *The only "hand-out" you need is at the end of your sleeve.*

Consider also that children live what they see. Even if you find yourself in that position, determine to work that much harder to ensure that your children see you making strides toward a better life. Show them that there are other neighborhoods and instill in them that if anyone has ever done it, they can do it too. Take them to neighborhoods and car dealerships so that they realize that there are other ways to live rather than relying on public assistance. Give them a vision of what their lives can be.

This is probably the toughest module of the whole system. Why? Because it is really hard to take an objective look at yourself and do the work consistently enough to see change. Part of changing your mindset, will be to look at your life like a movie. Not inserting yourself in it, but watching it objectively and giving attention to what's happening so that you can make adjustments and changes as needed.

You must change your mind to change your life. That is part of the reason that we have launched the Thousandaire Academy, to help you get your head right. This means you must develop a mental toughness that will allow you to overcome any obstacle.

**Katrina:**

*It was a long run, the Marine Corps Marathon. Trust me. I do not feel like I ever need to do it again. Three times a week, I would run three to five miles. On the weekend, it was a long six, eight, ten or 13 miles. Systematically, every weekend, running farther and farther and mentally preparing and getting ready to run the 26.2-mile marathon. The mental preparedness turned out to be the most important piece of this exercise. Being mentally ready, because at some point out there, it stopped being about my body; only my thinking kept me moving. About mile 16, you are like, "You know what? If I do not stay focused, if I am not mentally strong enough, I am not going to be able to finish this race." You have to overcome all of the thoughts, all of the things that are competing for your attention, and just keep moving forward. That is why being mentally prepared is important. You have got to be conditioned and mentally prepared for wealth and abundance. You have heard it said, "More money, more problems." In actuality, it is just a bigger set of problems. It is different than what you are experiencing now. Just prepare yourself. Let's get your head right so that ultimately, you can win.*

**Jai:**

In the 1990s, someone started promoting WWJD bracelets, and it became enormously popular. Many people were wearing them and were excited to show them off. For those who are not familiar, WWJD was the acronym for 'What Would Jesus Do?' It was used within the Evangelical Christian community as a reminder of their belief and demonstration of their faith in Jesus. I remember this movement resonating with me on so many levels.

I used this principle of 'What Would Jesus Do in other areas of my life by asking myself the question, 'What Would _____ Do?' in certain situations. (Insert someone you respect in the blank.) When presented with challenges, I would insert the name of the person I had respect for and believed had expertise and wisdom in the area of my concern. Before I made certain decisions, I would go through this exercise. I soon realized that what I was doing was forcing myself to think clearly and intentionally rather than acting impulsively. I was changing my philosophies and the way I thought about things. My approach was becoming different because I was creating an environment of thought consideration in my decision-making.

I began seeing people who had what I wanted and who were doing the things that I wanted to do. Again, I used the WWJD exercise to get a handle on what those successful, financially free people were doing. What books were they *reading, what seminars were they attending and who were they associating with?* These series of questions caused me, on one hand, to imagine the answer and go out and get the information I thought they were getting. On the other hand, when I could, I simply asked them what they were doing. Things started changing for me. I was becoming exposed to new information and new ways of thinking.

You see, something as simple as a bracelet from years ago had a major impact on me. The impact was on the way I thought, my mindset and the way I viewed my life. All of the major challenges and the solutions to those challenges in your life will begin with the way you think, and with your life's philosophies.

You can make money or you can make excuses, but you cannot do both. Controlling your thinking will also assist you in getting rid of the excuses, and making sure that you are not quitting. Being intentional about your purpose in life and walking toward your destiny is a powerful decision. Controlling your thinking and changing your mindset has everything to do with your overall success.

There is no minimum status level in order to start with the Thousandaire Academy. It doesn't matter how much you have, it only matters that you purpose to be a good steward of what you have. Whether it is your money, your clothes or your thinking, make the most of it.

A while back, there was a conversation that Katrina had with a spiritual mentor. In light of her then current situation and problems, the mentor asked how she was. Her response was "Fine, I have to be, I have no choice but to be fine." Her mentor stopped right there in the middle of the conversation and rebuked her saying, "Do not ever say that again. You always have options. If you allow yourself to believe that you do not have options, you will find yourself getting bitter and not better." We have to control how we frame our thoughts and situations. How you see them will determine whether you grow through them or simply go through them. Do not let the challenges of your process exist for no reason. One of Katrina's favorite philosophies and quotes is "Grow through what you go through, so your greatness can show through." At least then, you can be an example to others of what happens when you change your thinking and consequently change your life.

> *"Grow through what you go through so your greatness can show through."*

Many authors have shared thoughts on the principle that we are discussing here. "As a man thinketh in his heart, so is he" (Proverbs 23:7, KJV). There is even a book "As a Man Thinketh," by James Allen that the students of the Thousandaire Academy receive as part of the curriculum. These and other readings bring us to the following conclusions: If the life you live today is the sum total of the choices you made yesterday, and the choices you made yesterday were totally dependent on what you were thinking then, changing your thinking is the solution to the equation. Maybe what you've been taught to think was dependent on what someone said about you, what you say to yourself, environmental situations or something else. It's time to change the way you think about your life and your future. You are destined for more, so refuse to settle for less.

We are going to help you discover who you were created to be; embrace the fact that you are good and powerful and that you have a purpose and a destiny. You were created to solve a problem, and most often, solving this problem is the key to your achieving success and the wealth that comes with it. We are going to help you discover that so we can begin to move you systematically through the process of becoming a thousandaire, and ultimately, a millionaire.

> *In 2015, roughly 6 out of 10 (approximately 62 percent) of millennials (people ranging in age from 18 to 34) and 51 percent of people from Generation X (ages 35 to 50) said the U.S. has been successful because of its ability to change.*
> ***[Pew Research Center]***

# Chapter 2

## Have a Coach and a Mentor:
### It's Easier to Get There With Someone Who Knows the Way

A key to becoming financially independent is finding a mentor. It is amazing how often we find ourselves looking to people in our same condition—or worse—and expect them to give us information that will get us out of our situation. A broke person can only teach you how to be broke-er. If you are serious about getting money issues out of the way, you have to find someone who has already done it, and then do what he or she did. It is okay to be a copycat as long as you are copying the right cat (or 'Kat' as Katrina tells her coaching clients).

**Katrina:**

*If you do not know where you are, there is no way you are going to get where you want to go. In my car, my GPS has a name, it's Natasha. She's like a mentor to me because when I'm trying to get somewhere, she keeps me on the straight and narrow path; pointing out the fastest and most efficient route. I do not know what I would do without her. She also tells me, 'Oh, there is an accident or a delay on your current route—do not go that way.'* Then, she finds an alternate route and tells me how to self-correct so that I do not lose time en route to my destination. Natasha is always looking out for my best interest, and I always have a choice of whether to listen to her guidance or not. The question is: Do I listen to my mentor, Natasha, or do I go my own way and end up in that two-hour traffic jam and miss my flight? Ask me how I know about that...

In case you were wondering, there are clear differences between a mentor and a coach, which is why we need to have both. A mentor will share their own story, their own career path, as well as provide guidance, motivation, emotional support, role modeling and long-term direction. A mentor will pour into your life and guide you since they have already walked the path you are walking. Coaches give more day-to-day directions about how to complete specific tasks. Think of a *basketball coach* or a *football coach*. A coach is an expert in a certain skill and will teach you until you master it. Although a coach and the coached will have some relationship, it doesn't normally have the depth of a mentor's relationship with their mentee.

Mentoring is based on relationship. It becomes a safe environment for mentor and mentee to discuss issues, challenges, goals and more. It deals with intangibles like work/life balance, self-confidence and self-perception. Coaching as we stated above, deals with the more tangible issues and skill sets.

Most often, if you are being coached, it is for the short-term. The length of time that the coaching relationship lasts is totally based on the purpose of the relationship. Mentoring, however—in order to be successful—takes time. Most often, it takes a lot of time. To be in an effective mentoring relationship, each of the partners must learn one another, build a climate of trust and security so that there can be transparency. Coaching is designed to improve a skill or performance of a skill while mentoring is designed to develop an individual.

You have to have the right people around you that can help shorten the learning curve. Why would I go the long road and the long route around getting something done, when I have somebody right there who can tell me the steps to take in order to make it happen a lot easier and more quickly for me? Having a mentor in place is powerful to make that happen. If you want to have more money, then you need to find people who have more money than you do and study what they do. Remember, it is not just about asking questions, it is also about getting answers and applying what you learn in order to strengthen your position.

*A mentor is not someone whose advice you seek; a mentor is someone whose advice you listen to, and apply to your life.*

A major key to success in every area—not just your finances—is having a coach and a mentor in place from the beginning. Additionally, you want to hang around people who are going in the same direction that you are. We've all heard it said that associations are everything. If you hang around nine broke people, you are bound to be the tenth one. On the flip side of the same token, if you hang around nine wealthy, successful and confident people, you are bound to be the tenth one of those too.

> *"The best way to cut your learning curve and achieve a specific result is to find people who've already achieved what you want and then model their behavior. Rather than try to figure it all out on your own, find someone who has already achieved what you want, determine how this person did it, model this behavior and make it your own."*[4] -Hal Elrod

Jim Rohn, who has been called the father of the personal development industry, said that your income is the average of your five closest friends. (Some of us need new friends.) The bottom line is that you have to get away from those who have your problems and get around those who have your solutions.

Are you asking why would one of those wealthy, successful and confident people want to be around me even though I have not walked in my success as of yet? I am sure glad you asked that. You are right. If you are going to bring down someone's income average by being in their circle of

---

[4] Elrod, Hal. 7.1 Steps to Create Multiple Streams of Income. Entrepreneur.com. Jan. 22, 2015.

friends, they may not be as willing to invite you in. So how do you get there? There are several ways.

Respect is the master key to building and maintaining a solid relationship with a potential mentor. You have to respect them, respect their time and respect their wisdom. *A mentor is not someone whose advice you seek; a mentor is someone whose advice you listen to, and apply to your life.* If you trust a person enough to call them your mentor, then you absolutely should trust them enough to do what they say. Often we just go up to people and ask them to be our mentors. When you ask that of someone, you have to realize what you are asking them to commit to you and what you are committing to them. Basically, you are asking them to take the lessons that they have spent their entire life learning and give them to you at no cost and with no expectation of a return on their investment. This includes all of their ups and downs, successes and failures, triumphs and disappointments. This is incredibly selfish and short-sighted; and believe me, wealthy people are not wealthy because they are stupid or because they waste resources. You must identify and make known the value that you can bring to their lives as well.

If you want someone to mentor you, make it your business to pay attention to their lives. You are looking to discover an area where you can add value and fill a void. Create the plan and present it to them. When you are open to adding your gifting(s) to their vision, most successful people will be more open to inviting you in.

**Katrina:**

*One of my mentors in the network marketing industry did not do a lot of traveling when we first met. He was wildly successful on a local level, but had not yet branched out to the rest of the world. When I decided that I was going to be successful in that same company, I asked, if he would be willing to assist me. He agreed. That is when my work started. It was not about taking him to lunch and carrying his bags, although I did that. It was not about telling him what my goals and plans were, although I did that too. It was about finding a need (a void) in his life and filling it. I became his travel agent. Whenever he went anywhere, he would call me, and I would book his flights and hotel stays. I became invaluable to him. Here we are 15 years later, and we are still a part of each other's lives. Of course, we ultimately hired travel agents and assistants, but the initial relationship was built on mutual service and respect.*

> "...When you ask someone for help, you are implicitly asking him to place a bet on you. The more people you get to bet on you, the larger your network of investors and the shorter the odds." [5]
> ~Christopher Matthews, journalist and talk-show host

---

[5] Pincott, J. Success: *Advice for achieving your goals from remarkably accomplished people.* New York: Random House Inc., 2005.

**Katrina:**

Back in 1994, when I was only 9 years old (just kidding), my then husband and I traveled to Hawaii to attend a business leader's event. Now just to make it clear, we absolutely could not afford to be in Hawaii. We got there by the skin of our teeth and only had $50 to spend for the whole week. Now if you have ever been to Hawaii, you know that a gallon of milk costs close to $50. There was no way that two people were going to eat on $50 for an entire week. It did not matter though. Not because we had love for one another (although we did), it did not matter because we were on a mission. We knew that coming to this particular event was going to change our lives. It meant that we had to sacrifice, but it really did change our lives.

Most of the people at this event were multimillionaires who had made their money in different business industries. One such couple was from Washington State and had made millions in the health care industry. We felt led to invite them to lunch and they accepted. We got to a restaurant there at the hotel and sat down to lunch. Remember, we only had $50. They ordered and we told them that we were fasting. We interviewed them and wrote down everything they said while they ate. When the check came, we took the check and paid it. The wife started crying. She said that no one had honored them in that way in a very long time; and that was because most people saw them as being extremely wealthy and never offered to pay the check. We were so blessed by that, but more importantly, we stumbled on a principle that we have used our entire lives to find a way to support those whose success we wanted to imitate.

*Motivational speaker Les Brown is a mentor of mine. I met him at a convention center where he was doing a book signing, and I said to him, "I've been praying for a mentor." He then responded, after looking at me strangely, 'looks like your prayers have been answered.' I proceeded to tell him what I brought to the table and how I could help support him. He agreed, we exchanged numbers, and from that time to now, we have been friends. We are close enough that when my mother passed away, he came and spoke at her Celebration of Life service. There are many other instances where this principle has worked to get me access to some of the greatest people in the world. It is my honor and privilege to serve. The ensuing connections are simply an added benefit.*

*Every time I have been able to gain a mentor, in any area, it is because I have moved with confidence and self-assurance in my talents, gifts and ability to help busy people become more of what they need to be.*

*You can have access to other mentors, either in person or by phone, and you can gain a mentor by beginning to listen to their audio teachings and reading their books. There are mentors who are close and who are at a distance. For many, many years, Jim Rohn was a mentor of mine. Charlie Tremendous Jones was also a mentor of mine. I've only met each of them once, yet I considered them my mentors because I took the books and audios that they poured their lives into producing and spent time with them and mulled over their concepts and adopted some of their beliefs. That made them my mentors and made their experiences mine for the taking. With that in mind, together we began a track to personal development. Remember, you do not get in life what you want, you get in life what you are. The only way to ever have more is to become more. We become more when we find people who are more, read their books and listen to their audios and take it a step further... we actually APPLY what we learn there.*

> "Workplace mentors used to be older and higher up the ranks than their mentees. Not anymore. In an effort to school senior executives in technology, social media and the latest workplace trends, many businesses are pairing upper management with younger employees in a practice known as reverse mentoring. The trend is taking off at a range of companies, from tech to advertising."[6]
> Source: www.wsj.com

---

[6] Kwoh, Leslie. Reverse mentoring cracks workplace. www.wsj.com. Nov. 28, 2011.

# Chapter 3

## *Affirmations:*
### *Your Words are Powerful*

Words are the building blocks of our lives. They are powerful tools that we can use to build up an empire or tear down a legacy. In a manner of speaking, our thought-life is a toolbox, filled with equipment that enables us to construct or deconstruct various areas of our lives. The question becomes How will you use your tool(s)? What will you build with your words?

Most people are familiar with some of the basic tools that can be found in a toolbox: hammer, wrench, screwdriver, tape measure, etc. But let's not forget about some of the specialized tools—like a circular saw—that we only need in certain circumstances. Sometimes it's necessary for us to utilize our specialty tools to achieve the desired product. For example, you don't need a saw if you're simply attempting to drive a nail into a piece of wood. You don't need a drill if you're sawing a piece of lumber in half. Our words function like tools, requiring specific words to get desired results. There's an old saying, "If all you have is a hammer, every problem is a nail." In reality, every problem isn't the same, so we must diversify the tools in our toolbox in order to appropriately address the challenges we face. The aim of the Thousandaire Academy is to help you add the necessary tools to your toolbox, so that you can efficiently construct the financial reality you want.

When was the last time you conducted a "word audit" of your vocabulary? In other words, when did you last assess the types of words you are using to create the circumstances you desire? Think about how audits work. If a corporation announces an audit of its finances or bookkeeping records, people know what to expect. That means someone very good with numbers and accounting is going to review all the money that came in and all the money that went out. At the end of the audit, there should be a full reconciliation and record of every dollar earned and spent.

In terms of a "word audit," we need to get in the habit of accounting for every word we say and the impact of those words in our own lives—and in the lives of those around us. Do you regularly speak words that are contrary to God's word about your financial prosperity? Do you regularly express fear instead of faith; or hopelessness instead of hope? Now, we know that it's not possible to always be cheery and optimistic about every single situation, especially when things aren't working out the way you planned. However, it is a requirement for every conqueror in the Kingdom to speak words of truth and power. As a believer, that is your reasonable service.

Simply put, words build up and tear down. In order to achieve the destiny you desire, it may be necessary to change the way you speak regarding your life. If the words you use about your finances were a building, would the structure look more like a sand castle, a house of straw, a brick house, a high-rise building, the Leaning Tower of Pisa or the Taj Mahal? Sometimes it's helpful to make words into a picture to visualize what you're actually building with them.

*Death and life are in the power of the tongue.*

When you speak with a clear lack of faith and insincerity, you're essentially working to form a sand castle—something with no stability and no longevity. But when you're working on building a stone structure that can endure harsh environments and tough times—and become something that will last beyond your lifetime—then you're using words of power that last. That's the result of speaking strong words with strong conviction, based on faith in God's promises. Part of the building process is having a blueprint, and that's what this book will help you to do—build a blueprint for your financial success that shows you step-by-step how to build something that will last.

In your quiet, alone time, what do you say to yourself? What do people that surround you say about you? If the words that you spoke came out of your mouth and wrapped themselves around you like clothing, what kind of self-talk wardrobe would you be wearing? Could you stand to be around yourself? (Adapted from Jesus, CEO, author Laurie Beth Jones).

**Jai:**

*I have a friend that simply frustrates us with his words. Great guy, I love him dearly, but this guy is so negative that if he goes into a dark room he starts to develop. I have to limit the amount of time that I interact with him because the son-of-a-gun is just negative all the time. "How are you doing?" "Terrible, terrible." "What are you doing?" "Nothing, just waiting for the hearse to come." I am sure that you can relate to this, because everyone knows a Negative Nancy. If your name is Nancy, I'm sorry, if you are not negative. You know what I am saying, right? Just really negative all the time. I have heard people like that, whether on the job or anywhere else or in our families. We have to surround ourselves with positivity which means we must avoid negativity. People do all of this negative talking and wonder why their lives are so messed up.*

Your words not only impact you and your personal reputation—shaping how other people perceive you—but let's not forget the effect that your words have on others. What immediately comes to mind is the tone we use with our children and how we prepare them for the future. It's often said that children are like little sponges, soaking up everything around them that they see and hear. What are your children learning and hearing from you based on your words? What seeds are you sowing into their lives that will take root and grow? Do you often speak in negative, condescending ways that discourage and weigh down your kids? Have you ever shot down their dreams by telling them something was impossible, or discouraged them from pursuing something just because it was different or difficult? It's so easy to discount childhood dreams as unrealistic fantasies, but let's not forget that children are gifts from God, and our responsibility is to nourish and nurture their dreams and aspirations. Negative words have the ability to suffocate dreams, to the point that they never revive or recover.

Translations of the scripture that says, 'What you do unto the least of these, you do unto me' indicate that Jesus is referring to our protection and treatment of children; the smallest and most vulnerable individuals in our society. We have a moral obligation not only to protect and provide for our children, but also to protect and defend their dreams by offering guidance and safe havens for them to spread their wings. They will be listening, watching and following our example. Let's make sure the words we use are empowering and encouraging for ourselves and others.

> *To achieve our dreams we need roots to stand and wings to fly.*

We all need two things to help toward achieving our dreams: roots and wings. We believe every individual needs to know and understand his or her heritage. He needs to know who he is and where he comes from; why he is the way he is and what he is capable of accomplishing. When you think of a big, tall tree, we look at the tree and only see half of it. We see the trunk, the bark, the branches and leaves. What we do *not* see is the roots, which make up the other half of the tree. The roots are what keep the tree standing. The roots help the tree to survive the strong wind and storms. The roots keep the tree alive and healthy, and provide the nourishment needed to grow taller and stronger. The tree cannot survive without its roots. As a matter of fact, without the roots, there is no tree.

We all need to know our roots, because the roots will help sustain us in the winds and storms of life. Deep roots have the ability to stabilize and strengthen families. Our faith, family and community roots are the unseen half of the tree that keeps us grounded and helps us survive through life's ups and downs. Roots give us a sense of belonging and a sense of security. Roots bring clarity to purpose and provide a guiding direction in our lives. Also, letting our young people know about their roots will give them pride in who they are and help them grow into the next generation of leaders that we need.

Perhaps you have heard the story of the Chinese bamboo tree. It is a lesson about patience, perseverance and the importance of having deep roots. One year, a young farmer was given some seeds to plant and grow his garden. Every day, he diligently tended the garden, taking great care to root out the weeds, fertilize and water the plants. In a few weeks, all the plants except for one began to grow and sprout and produce small seedlings that would one day become a harvest. The one plant that showed no progress at all was the

Chinese bamboo tree. The farmer was not discouraged. Even though the bamboo tree showed no signs of life—much less growth—he continued to fertilize, weed and water it just like all the other plants. He did this for a whole year, yet the bamboo tree did not grow an inch. By now, the other plants had grown, produced bountiful fruits and vegetables, and it was time for the second year of planting. Still, there was nothing from the bamboo tree.

Every now and then, the farmer considered digging up the bamboo tree to see what was going on, but he didn't. He just learned to be patient and to trust that the plant would grow in due time. In the meantime, the farmer kept the weeds out of the garden and made sure all the other plants received plenty of sunshine and water. Year after year, the farmer grew a beautiful garden, and was able to provide food for his family and even sell extra in the marketplace. Still, the bamboo tree remained unchanged. Three years passed. Four years passed. Finally, in the fifth year, something amazing happened. The bamboo tree that had remained unchanged for four years, grew an amazing 80 feet tall in the fifth year. During the previous four years, the Chinese bamboo tree actually had been growing, but it was growing its roots downward in the ground, so that the tree would be able to support its phenomenal growth out of the ground later. Without the four years of growing its roots, the bamboo tree would not be able to survive and thrive. The same is true about us.

Once we have our roots established, we also need to be given wings to fly, to learn, to grow and explore. Wings—literally and philosophically—allow people to soar. They can fly high above limitations into the possibilities of their own potential when the boundaries and limits are removed and they are encouraged to do more and become more than what they see. Education provides wings. Exposure to new people, places and circumstances grows wings. Encouraging words, along with the financial tools we need, are other forms to develop our wings.

When we fail to develop our wings, then we are limited to performing below our capabilities and potential; much like the fabled eagle who was raised as a chicken. A story is told about a baby bird that fell from its nest and was discovered by a farmer who raised chickens. Fearful that the bird would not survive alone, the farmer placed it in the coop for safety and raised it with the rest of the chickens. Although it was obvious the baby bird was different—much bigger and stronger—the chickens accepted him as one of their own and treated him just like all the other chickens. During breakfast, lunch and dinner, the baby bird that had been rescued could be seen scratching the ground, strutting around the farm, and pecking in the grass for bugs and worms—just like all the other chickens.

One day, a majestic eagle was flying overhead. The baby bird happened to look up and was astonished by what he saw. He ran to tell his chicken family, "Do you see that bird up in the sky? One day I'm going to fly and soar just like him." The chickens clucked and laughed. "Don't be silly," they said. "That's an eagle. You're a chicken, and chickens don't fly. Get your head out of the clouds. You'll never be an eagle like that." The baby bird was disappointed by what they said, but believed it to be true. He went back to scratching and pecking in the dust – just like the rest of the chickens.

Several more weeks went by, and once again, the baby bird looked up in the sky and saw the same majestic eagle flying overhead. He was mesmerized by how high the eagle was flying and how wide his wings were spread, and stared into the sky, watching the eagle glide in the wind. It just so happened, that the farmer who had saved the baby bird saw him looking into the sky and realized that this was no ordinary chicken. He walked over to the bird, picked him up and carried him to a fence post near the chicken coop. The farmer said, "I believe you're an eagle, spread your wings and fly." The other chickens watched closely and began to cluck and cackle. They were convinced the baby bird was a chicken and that he could never fly. When the baby bird looked over and saw the chickens in the coop watching and heard them clucking, he lost his nerve and didn't even try to fly. He struggled off the fence post, flapped his way back to the ground and continued scratching around in the dust.

Fortunately, the farmer knew better. He packed up the baby bird and put him in his truck and drove several miles out onto the hillside – out of sight of the chickens and the coop. With the baby bird safely tucked under his arms, the farmer climbed the tallest tree he could find and said, "Little bird, you are not a chicken; you are an eagle and eagles are meant to soar." He lifted the baby bird into the air and released him; instantly and instinctively, the eagle knew how to fly. Within minutes, the baby eagle was soaring high in the clouds and never returned to the chicken coop. After all, he was an eagle and eagles are meant to fly. The best thing we can do for ourselves and for each other is to establish strong roots to stand, and powerful wings to fly.

One of the best defenses against a negative mindset is Affirmative Language. For the purposes of the Thousandaire Academy, we will define Affirmative Language as words and expressions that emphasize optimism and reinforce positive results when shared. In practice, Affirmative Language is the exact opposite of Negative Language. In using our words, we affirm—or underscore the positive reality—our perspective on life and its surrounding circumstances.

If you are already in the habit of using negative words about your life and finances, it's easy to forget the power and effect of those words. In actuality, sometimes we do not realize that we are not broke. We are just simply "POOR" – meaning that we are P-O-O-R: **P**assing **O**ver **O**pportunities **R**epeatedly and **P**utting **O**bstacles **O**ver **R**iches. Why? Because we've not had anyone to teach us how to recognize a good opportunity; or maybe we are poor because our priorities and perspective is out of line, and we are elevating obstacles over riches. That means we are allowing things, situations and what people have said about us to get in our way. We can deal with all of that in the affirmation process.

However, someone needs to be listening to what you say and help you wage a war against the negativity.

A young lady that we spoke with commented, "I am broke." Our response: "No, you just do not have the money yet." See the shift in that? That is powerful, because what that tells us in the subconscious is that the money's coming. It may not be here right now, but it is on its way. Versus, "I am broke." Affirmations are powerful.

In our daily lives and businesses, the Bible is our guide in understanding what our financial priorities should be. The Bible is God's word for humankind and our existence in this world. We need look no further than the Bible for the perfect example of the power of words. In the beginning, God literally used His words to speak the world into existence; His Creation. (Genesis 1) Then, further in the chapter, verse 26 says, "He has given us dominion over all the earth (emphasis ours)." That means that we have the same rights and authority through Christ to "create" the existence we want to see materialize. Not only did He speak Creation; He also spoke blessings and destiny upon the lives of countless figures throughout scripture. In the book of Job 22:28, we read the words: "Thou shalt also decree a thing, and it shall be established unto thee: and the light shall shine upon thy ways." Numerous other translations loosely paraphrase the scripture to say: 'When you declare and decide on something, it will happen, and light will shine on your ways.' Think about what that means for us today. All we need to do is make up our minds that we want something specific to happen (in accordance with God's Will), and it will happen. Not only that, after it happens, the continued work we do will be illuminated and blessed. That is nothing short of miraculous!

The books of Matthew and Luke both tell us that the mouth only speaks from what's within the heart. So, if we want to change our words and their results, we also need to consider what's in our hearts. Do you have a heart for the things of God? Do you have a heart that longs to help others develop and grow? Do you have a heart for good, or a heart that wishes evil upon others? Those are tough, but important questions to answer. If the words that consistently come out of your mouth are inconsistent with the love of God, then the issue isn't just your words, the issue is your heart. Neither one of us is a medical doctor, but if your life isn't what you want it to be, then maybe it's time for you to receive a heart transplant. It is the Great Physician alone who has the ability to change both hearts and minds. If you sincerely desire to change the trajectory of your life, the answer is only one prayer away.

Pray this prayer with us:

*"Dear God, You said in Your Word that if I acknowledge that You raised Jesus from the dead, and that I accept Him as my Lord and Savior, I would be saved and become part of your family. Lord, I believe You raised Jesus from the dead and that He rose again on the third day. I accept Him now as my personal Lord and Savior. I accept my salvation from sin right now. I am now saved. Jesus is my Lord. Jesus is my Savior. Thank you, Father God, for forgiving me, for saving me, and giving me eternal life with You.*

*Now Lord, please create in me a clean heart and renew a right spirit within me. Your Word also says that out of the abundance of the heart the mouth speaks. Help me to speak works of encouragement, words of blessings, and of peace and life. Let others see You within me, and may your purpose for me be revealed. In all things I will give thanks, everything with a grateful heart. In Jesus name I pray. Amen.*

A spiritual heart transplant is going to set off a chain reaction of events in your life. Once your heart is no longer hardened, it will immediately affect how you feel and what you think about. Once your thoughts change, your emotions will follow their leading. After you allow your mind and feelings to be changed, then as a matter of course, the words that you say will be different. Your words will begin to reflect His Word. In essence, the heart changes the mind, which alters the words that are spoken and the consequences that result.

Now, that you are out of heart surgery and rehabilitation—and on the road to recovery—let's go back to the toolbox and construction site. Imagine now that every word you say is a building block that immediately manifests in front of your eyes. Imagine what would happen when you say the words: "This job is driving me crazy!" or "I'm so broke, I can't even pay attention." Think about how you would feel if you woke up tomorrow morning and had literally gone crazy because of your words. You would no longer be able to think straight or make decisions. Everything you did or said would be illogical and incoherent—all because of your words. What does it even mean to be so broke that you can no longer pay attention? That would mean that you had no finances and no resources. That means no cash on hand; no money in the bank; no money in savings, investments or retirement; no one you could call to help you out; and no way to get the help you needed. Basically, all you would have in terms of finances are the words in your mouth. We're guessing that if the things you repeatedly said started happening immediately, it would serve as great motivation to start thinking before you speak—and to consider what you're actually saying before you allow those negative things to come out of your mouth.

Now, envision the results of Affirmation Language in your life. You routinely say things like: "Nothing can stop me from achieving my goals," or "I have everything I need to be successful, and I am blessed to be an example and a blessing to others." Just watch the financial pillars in your life bond together to build something great for you and your loved ones. The immediate manifestation of your words would not only begin to build a financial legacy for your family, but also would build your confidence and reputation, serving as an encouragement to those around you.

# Chapter 4

## Notations:
## Have a Written Plan with Checkpoints

"Write the vision, and make it plain on tablets, so he may run who reads it." (Habakkuk 2:2)

In the Thousandaire Academy, there are notations or notes that you will need to make along this journey. You are going to have to write down what it is that you want to have. You are going to have to begin to journal or chronicle your thoughts and actions. When you take something out of your head and put it on paper, it becomes more real. It also gives you a place to go back to, so that when life happens, and your emotions begin to get in the way, you can remind yourself that your dreams are going to come true.

You can literally go back to that journal. You can go back to that piece of paper. You can go back to that dream board or dream book. Then, without the emotion attached, you can clearly see what it is that you are planning, and where it is that you are going. Again, if you do not have those things written down, and if you haven't made it plain, then others are not going to be able to run with you to help bring it to pass.

Visions are holistic in how they work. They outline the big picture and help identify who we need on board to get stuff done. Not only must you have a plan for yourself, but you must also have a plan for who is going to help you accomplish it. When you are planning to elevate your life, opportunities and status, the harsh reality is that sometimes everyone around you now cannot go with you. It doesn't mean you don't love them or that they are not important to you. It means that what got you here won't necessarily get you there. Part of Thousandaire Academy requires a Life Audit, where we do an assessment of where we are—and where we want to go. Taking part in this academy of learners, dreamers and doers will guide you to a deeper understanding of what it takes to get what you want.

In addition, the plan will provide direction on the types of mentors and professional relationships that you need to cultivate in order to grow. It also points out some people who may be in your life that are not helpful or beneficial to what you're trying to accomplish. If we were to ask if there's anyone in your circle of influence who is negative or skeptical about your potential for success, one or two people would probably come to mind immediately. That's unfortunate, but definitely not uncommon. These people—whether family or friends—may have a role to play in your life, but not a role to play in your success. You owe it to yourself to identify the negative naysayers and "bid them adieu" in terms of planning for your future. Should you invite them to the backyard barbecue? Absolutely. Should you discuss your financial plans and dreams and solicit their input? Absolutely not. In the process of writing your vision and making it plain, you should also be very clear about who is (and is not) going to be a part of that plan and what role(s) you would like them to play.

How many times have you heard someone talk about their great idea, and then say that the details are all in their head? We encounter countless people with big dreams, but no plan. In their minds, they have the perfect product, a life-changing idea or a novel concept that everybody needs and no one else has thought of. When they are asked about their plan for moving forward, there is only silence—because they have no plan. Rather, the response is said while pointing to their head, "It's all up here." The problem with having "it all up here" is that no one else can see or read and understand it so that they know what to do. We have clear biblical instructions about writing the vision and making it plain for a reason; and the reason is so that others can access the necessary information and details to implement the vision. If you have an idea that you've been formulating in your head, the Thousandaire Academy will help you take it from the concept stages and direct you toward creating a business or marketing plan to get it moving. That is one of many tools available to participants as part of the accountability required to move to the next level.

> *"Goals 'held' in the mind are more likely to be jumbled up with the other 1,500 thoughts per minute that the average human being experiences."*[7] -Goalband.co.uk. 2014

Let's talk about checkpoints and timelines. Even if you have a good, written plan, it's worthless unless it is accompanied by specific metrics and benchmarks and deadlines. Yes, you are going to do something great, but when are you going to do it, and how will you know it's done? Metrics in our planning process help us stay on track and ensure that we're making meaningful progress. If there are certain steps you need to take before you can accomplish something, then the plan will help you to stay on schedule in completing those tasks. For example, before you quit your job to work full time on your entrepreneurial venture, some checkpoints might include paying off any credit card debt and accumulating a certain amount of money in your savings account. Another example might be to max out the college savings plan for your own children before investing thousands of dollars toward building a school overseas for disadvantaged children. Even if your objective is a good one, it still must occur at the proper time and in the proper sequence of your God-given priorities. To take it one step further, whatever your goals might be, those goals are also accompanied by specific dates in which the items need to be

---

[7] 18 Facts About Goals and Their Achievement. Goalband.co.uk. 2014.

completed. Once they are done, you can check them off your task list and move on to the next thing.

People underestimate what it takes to start and finish a project. So many people start working on something with really good intentions. Then, it gets increasingly more difficult, or they don't get the results they want as quickly as they want, and they begin to get discouraged. It's easy to quit, and many people do. In the Thousandaire Academy, we want to equip you with the skill sets you need to face challenges and overcome the odds and to keep moving forward.

**Katrina:**

*One of the things I noticed as I have travelled around the world extensively for business and ministry is how many unfinished building projects I have seen. There were unfinished houses, office buildings, business parks and even schools that got started, but were never finished. There was scaffolding around buildings with no walls, or wooden structures with no roofs that had been works in progress for years. The most common explanation for most of them is that they ran out of money. For others, there was no original plan, just energy and excitement over getting started—with no vision or blueprint for how to finish. That is why the Bible instructs us to first count the cost for whatever it is we are attempting to do. (Luke 14:28-30) Counting the cost is just another way of saying, write the vision and make it plain. You have to know what it takes to get where you want to go.*

*It all starts with a self-assessment. You have to know where you are. This is the part where you really have to be* honest with yourself, good, bad, or ugly; here is where I am, and this is my current financial picture. This is not about beating yourself up or putting yourself down; it's just an honest assessment of where you really are. This is important to formulate the road map and make sense of what needs to be adjusted.

A Thousandaire Academy notebook is the first mile-marker in your personal financial road map. As you begin to understand things like the Rule of 72 and compounding interest (The Rule of 72 is a shortcut to estimate the number of years required to double your money at a given annual rate of return), you will want to make some adjustments that keep you on track. Understand and appreciate the differences between a bank and a credit union, and how you can use and leverage each of them. Where's the best place to get a loan? How do I negotiate the best terms? Those are just some of things that you will want to know early on.

As you prepare to get started, are there some bad financial habits that you need to change or drop? Do you waste money on things that add no value to your life? Do you have monthly recurring credit card charges for products or services that you don't actually use? Are you paying too much for convenience, when it's simpler and more cost-effective to do things a little differently (e.g. purchasing bottled water instead of refilling a water bottle). This entire process will be easier to manage if you make the commitment to drop poor financial habits on the front-end. Ridding yourself of these habits will free up additional resources and make it easier to incorporate new and improved habits into your routine.

Next, as you prepare to get started, will be accountability. Numerous studies indicate a higher likelihood for success when we are accountable to another individual or a group for the steps we are going to take. Accountability reminds us that people are watching to see if what we do aligns with what we say we are going to do. It's the process of finalizing a plan, making it accessible to others who will be assisting, and then asking them to challenge us along the way to make sure we are making notable progress toward our goals. Think about how easy it is to quit doing something that's hard if no one else knows you are doing it anyway. For example, if you make a commitment to your family to eat healthier and you share that commitment with everyone in the house, you're much less likely to fry up bacon, eggs and a stack of pancakes after saying you plan to eat fruit and yogurt every day. It's basic human nature in that our behavior adapts when we know that others are watching.

Begin with these notations below to help keep you on track. When life happens—and it will—these notes will serve as a constant reminder to remain focused and to keep your priorities straight. (In the absence of the official Thousandaire Academy Notebook, get a notebook dedicated to this process and begin to make notes on your finances.) Each section of the notebook should correspond with the following labels:

- My WHY for Financial Success -- anyone can achieve the success they desire if they have this very important and key piece of information that sets kings apart from paupers. Be honest. Why do you need more money? What will you do with it when you get it? What are your intentions and your motives for embarking on this new financial journey? Write it down as a positive Affirmation.

- My Assets – write down everything that you own. Be sure to include property, real estate, bank accounts, savings accounts, retirement accounts, money under the mattress, insurance policies, etc.

- My Liabilities (Debts) – write down everything that you owe and everyone that you owe it to, along with the corresponding interest rates, balances and minimum payments. Although we always hear about eliminating debt, believe it or not, there is a time when debt's not completely bad, because you can leverage debt for another purpose. That means you are leveraging it to do something that is going to move you exponentially toward a more positive and larger financial goal. Being in debt is not always bad. It just depends on how you are using debt and whether you are controlling the debt or the debt is controlling you. There is actually strategy behind debt that can help you increase your net worth. If you are just in debt willy-nilly because you choose not to control your impulsive spending, that is a totally different situation. Understanding creative debt is imperative to your financial future. It's one of many topics we explain and explore in-depth in Thousandaire Academy.

- My Spending – write down everything that you spend for 30 days. A software program or mobile app that tracks this would work as well. This will serve as the beginning of your Strategic Spending Plan. Any wealth plan is going to include a strategic spending plan. A budget is really just a strategic spending plan. For some, the word budget makes them throw up their hands in resignation. We hate budgets, but a spending plan, we can live with. With your strategic spending plan in place, you know exactly how much you can spend on a weekly basis, because the ultimate deal is that we are trying to save some money, put some money together to invest, and now start having your money work for you instead of you only just working for your money.

- My Credit Score (from all 3 credit bureaus) – Become familiar with your credit scores and all applicable credit limits. You want to know how much credit you have and what percentage of that credit is available for you to leverage. The more available credit you have, the more advantageous it is to you for pursuing bigger and better opportunities in wealth creation.

You can request a free annual credit report, which will help clarify where you stand and what areas you need to work on and which accounts may still have balances. If there are mistakes or discrepancies, you should immediately contact the credit bureaus and provide proof of payment or confirmation for errors that need to be corrected. Below you will find contact information for the three major credit reporting agencies:

**Equifax Credit Information Services, Inc.**
P.O. Box 740256
Atlanta, GA 30374
(800) 685-1111
www.Equifax.com

**Experian**
P.O. Box 4500
Allen, TX 75013
(888) 397-3742
www.Experian.com

**TransUnion, LLC**
P.O. Box 2000
Chester, PA 19022
(800) 888-4213
www.Transunion.com

Alternatively, should you want a one-stop location for all three credit reports, visit www.AnnualCredit.com.

- My Investments -- Are you already in a position to invest? One of the worst things that could ever happen to somebody is to know a little bit of information that ultimately leads them down the wrong path. If you are not doing your research and making informed decisions, you're actually just gambling away your money. We need look no further than the Bible to see that investing is a scriptural principle. The parable of the talents provides an excellent narrative about what is expected of us as stewards of God's resources. When we are blessed with resources (e.g. time, talent and finances), the expectation is that we will not simply sit on those assets for the purpose of hoarding them, but rather that we will find a way to grow them and extend their usage.

- My Taxes – are you paying the minimum amount of taxes? As you learn more about this area, be prepared to reassess the last 3 years of your federal and state tax filings. Taxes, taxes, taxes. This is one of the little foxes that spoils the entire vine for so many Americans. More than likely, you are paying too much in taxes. There are two tax systems: one for the business owner and another for the employee. Even if you have a job, and there is nothing wrong with a job, you have got to understand the strategies available so that you legally pay the minimal amount of taxes due. So many people say, "Oh, at tax time, I am going to get a big 'ole refund." That is not exciting. You should not be getting a big refund at tax time because that means you've been unnecessarily loaning your hard-earned money to Uncle Sam. Focus on how to avoid that situation and better ways to use your money, so that you can generate interest on the money that you'll save and invest. Yes, you have to pay Caesar... give Caesar what's his, but you shouldn't give him a penny more than you absolutely must.

## My Monthly Budget

**Money Coming In**

☐ Primary Job  ☐ Child Support/Alimony

☐ Secondary/Part-time Job  ☐ Rental Income

☐ Disability/Social Services  ☐ Other _____

Total Monthly Household Income

$ _____

**Money Going Out**

| | |
|---|---|
| Tithes (10%) | $ _____ |
| Rent/Mortgage | $ _____ |
| Utilities | $ _____ |
|     -Water bill | |
|     -Gas bill | |
|     -Electric bill | |
| Groceries | $ _____ |
| Day/Childcare | $ _____ |
| Automobile(s) | $ _____ |
| Auto Insurance | $ _____ |
| Home/Renters Insurance | $ _____ |
| Telephone | $ _____ |
| Mobile Phone/Data | $ _____ |
| Student Loans | $ _____ |
| Credit Cards | $ _____ |
| Miscellaneous | $ _____ |
| Other (list) | $ _____ |
| **Total Monthly Expenses** | $ _____ |

## FINANCIAL SELF-ASSESSMENT

| | |
|---|---|
| 1. What is your WHY for financial success? | |
| 2. What is the total value of all your assets? | |
| 3. What is the total of all your liabilities? | |
| 4. What is your current total net worth (your assets, minus your liabilities)? | |
| 5. What is your monthly household budget? | |
| 6. What are your three credit scores? | a. Equifax<br>b. Experian<br>c. TransUnion |
| 7. What is the current tax rate you're paying? | _____ % |
| 8. What is the annual total of your investment income? | |

| FINANCIAL ASSESSMENT cont'd | |
|---|---|
| 9. Describe your short-term (1-year) financial goals: | |
| 10. Describe your long-term (10-year) financial goals: | |

**Execute and Regularly Review Your Plan.** Already, you are making progress. You've spent all this time creating the plan, and you have gotten your mind right. You have looked under the hood and figured out where you want to go. You have looked at the good, bad and the ugly and finally, you have a good road map together. Now let's get it done. Let's execute on the plan.

There was a lady we met in Jacksonville, Florida, at a 3-day event where we were presenting and talking about what we were working on and what we were doing. When she came back the next day, she handed over an envelope. Inside was her pay stub and credit report, along with other crucial financial documents. She said, "Please, just tell me what to do. Tell me what to do. I will do it. I will learn it. I will read it. I just need help." We were pleased to help her, and we're ready to offer that same help to you.

The key is reviewing your own plan on a consistent basis and knowing exactly where you stand and what your financial picture is. It is just a check point. You have to make sure that you are progressing. The best way to do that as you execute the plan is to make sure that you have your check-ins, whether they are on a weekly, monthly, and/or quarterly basis. That's how it needs to work in any business, and in your personal business of You, Inc.

Even NASA has course corrections. Did you know that when a rocket ship takes off, it often is not even headed on the right path towards its goal? As a matter of fact, it is off track more than 97 percent of the time. The crew has to check in constantly with the home base in Houston. You know what that means? "Houston, we have a problem." We've heard that phrase in movies and as the punch line of a lot of jokes. Well for good reason, because that is what's really going on. Houston is saying, "No, go this way. No, make this adjustment. No, make this course correction." In response to the constant adjustments, ultimately, that rocket ship lands on the moon or wherever it is intended to go. Without those regular check-ins, who knows where they would end up? Without these check-ins, who knows where you will end up? Because we know your goal, we are going to make sure that you land as close to that mark as you are willing to work for.

Decide right now where you want to go. Maybe you're saying, "Well, okay, I want to do better financially." No, you're going to need to think harder than that and get into the details. There is something powerful about specificity. There is something about zeroing in on where you want to go and then drafting a timeline that gets you there. It's time to ask and answer: "Where do I want to go in my life from a financial standpoint? What does that picture look like? And what is the next step I need to take to make it happen?"

## 1-Year Financial Plan

| Financial Goal | Details & Deadline | Status |
|---|---|---|
|  |  |  |
| Ex: Pay off $5,000 credit card debt | •10 months or October 1, 2017<br>•Pay an extra $500 per month toward debts | Savings plan in Progress.<br><br>Month 1 of 10 |
|  |  |  |
|  |  |  |
|  |  |  |
|  |  |  |
|  |  |  |

Your Commitment Signature

_____

Date

Witness Signature

_____

Date

## 5-Year Financial Plan

| Financial Goal | Details & Deadline | Status |
|---|---|---|
| | | |
| Ex: Build investment portfolio to $100,000 in 5 annual stages | Retire all personal debts in 2 years – December 31, 20____ Adopt "aggressive" investment strategy through risk diversification by March 30, 20____ | Steps 1-3 of financial portfolio expansion complete |
| | | |
| | | |
| | | |

Your Commitment Signature

_____

_____
Date

Witness Signature

_____

_____
Date

## 10-Year Financial Plan

| Financial Goal | Details & Deadline | Status |
|---|---|---|
|  |  |  |
| Ex: Pay off primary home mortgage |  |  |
|  |  |  |
|  |  |  |
|  |  |  |
|  |  |  |
|  |  |  |
|  |  |  |
|  |  |  |

Your Commitment Signature          Witness Signature

_____          _____

_____          _____

Date                                                         Date

# Chapter 5

## Generational Wealth Choices:
### Leaving a Legacy

How do you want to be remembered? When you are no longer physically here to represent yourself, what is it that you want people to say about you or to remember about you? When your impact on your family, neighborhood, community or the world is discussed, what will people acknowledge? Will they be proud or embarrassed? Will it make them want to laugh or cry? Is it a legacy they can build on to inspire others, or is it something they hope fades into the past? Those are some of the considerations of those committed to building the Kingdom when contemplating the contributions they will both make and leave to world. Those are the questions people ask when they are planning to leave a legacy.

Let's discuss that idea more. Leaving a legacy. What does that mean to you and for those who love you? Let's start with this question: What legacy are you currently building? What foundations are currently being laid and what is the reputation that you have right now? Is it the one you want, or is now a good time to change directions?

Define your own destiny. The people with the best choices in life are the ones who create their own options. Long gone are the days of 30-year retirement parties, gold watches and rewards for company loyalty. We're now deeply entrenched in the "dog-eat-dog" days where enterprising corporate warriors 'take no prisoners and eat the wounded.' The keys to leaving a powerful personal legacy are to reinvent and reinforce your relevance in the marketplace, to reach new audiences, and to increase your value to existing ones. You may need to forge a new path where one doesn't exist, so that you can create the kind of wealth that allows you to make a difference and change the world. There is so much need in the world, the opportunities to make a positive difference are literally overflowing.

*Define your own destiny.*

There is a website titled DoSomething.org. On the site is an article titled "11 Facts About Global Poverty." Here is the list of those 11 facts. Consider this information through the lens of the Bible in Matthew 25:40, which states that what you do unto the "least of these" (the poor, humble, impoverished and forgotten individuals) you do unto the Lord.

**"Welcome to DoSomething.org, one of the largest orgs for young people and social change! After you've**

**browsed the 11 facts (with citations at the bottom), take action and volunteer with our millions of members. Sign up for a campaign and make the world suck less." (DoSomething.org)**

1. Nearly 1/2 of the world's population — more than 3 billion people — live on less than $2.50 a day. More than 1.3 billion live in extreme poverty — less than $1.25 a day.

2. 1 billion children worldwide are living in poverty. According to UNICEF, 22,000 children die each day due to poverty.

3. 805 million people worldwide do not have enough food to eat. Food banks are especially important in providing food for people that can't afford it themselves. Run a food drive outside your local grocery store so people in your community have enough to eat. Sign up for Supermarket Stakeout.

4. More than 750 million people lack adequate access to clean drinking water. Diarrhea caused by inadequate drinking water, sanitation, and hand hygiene kills an estimated 842,000 people every year globally, or approximately 2,300 people per day.

5. In 2011, 165 million children under the age 5 were stunted (reduced rate of growth and development) due to chronic malnutrition.

6. Preventable diseases like diarrhea and pneumonia take the lives of 2 million children a year who are too poor to afford proper treatment.

7. As of 2013, 21.8 million children under 1 year of age worldwide had not received the three recommended doses of vaccine against diphtheria, tetanus and pertussis.

8. 1/4 of all humans live without electricity — approximately 1.6 billion people.

9. 80% of the world population lives on less than $10 a day.

10. Oxfam estimates that it would take $60 billion annually to end extreme global poverty--that's less than 1/4 the income of the top 100 richest billionaires.

11. The World Food Programme says, "The poor are hungry and their hunger traps them in poverty." Hunger is the number one cause of death in the world, killing more than HIV/AIDS, malaria, and tuberculosis combined.

That information makes it really difficult to complain about what we don't have. This knowledge makes it very easy to find ways that you can help. In this chapter, we'll focus more on generational wealth choices and the ability of wealth creation to shape and uplift the world.

***Riches vs. Wealth:*** *A 2012 article posted by personal finance blogger Tyrone Solee states: Being rich and being wealthy seems to be synonymous as both involves having a lot of money. However, there's a big difference between the two. If you notice, there are a lot of so-called 'get-rich-quick' schemes but there are no 'get-wealthy-quick' schemes. The main difference between being rich and being wealthy is knowledge.*

> *Wealthy people know how to make money while rich people only have money. Rich people are motivated by money but wealthy people are motivated by their dreams, purpose and passion. Most rich people make a lot of money with their paychecks but the moment they stop working, they also stop making money. Being wealthy is defined as that status of an individual's existing financial resources that supports his or her way of living for a longer duration, even if he or she does not physically work to generate a recurring income.*

Project Thousandaire and the Thousandaire Academy are all about thinking forward. The whole concept is about making sure that the people who are coming behind us can follow in our footsteps and expand upon the work we started. We are setting the stage for them. It all boils down to the decisions that we make here, now, today. We are either teaching people to expect a handout or teaching them that the only hand they need is the one at the end of their sleeve. A mentor of ours used to say all the time, "The reason why some folks know what their great great great grandfather looked like and his picture is over the mantle is because he actually left them something." Some do not know who they are or even their names because nothing really happened to enhance or change their lives from the life of that person.

The point is that money is not everything (although some say it ranks up there with air), nor is it the only thing. The idea is that there were some things that great great great grandpa did in some families that set them up for generations down the road; something that they would always remember because he or she had the foresight to see, 'If I do something right now, I can set this up so those who follow me will be blessed because of something I did today.' It's not just about money, but also about mindset. If you have the right mindset, you can always get more money. As you think about your life, future and legacy, we also want you to think about the next generations and the foundation that you're laying for them to build upon.

We like to call that "cathedral thinking." When there is a very detailed cathedral being built, the architect and builders often realize they won't live to see the end result. But, they keep building. They build with the intention of laying the groundwork for those who come after them and will continue the work. Generational wealth will be created by our cathedral thinking. Let's stop thinking about what we need today. Stop thinking about, "Well, I need a new television. It is Black Friday, so I need to get outside and wait until Wal-Mart opens to get that good price." Why not just create more income? We've got to change our thinking to achieve generational wealth.

At some point, we have to make decisions about our finances that are based on situations and scenarios that are bigger than we are. Yes, we are talking about making choices that are based on the generations to come. Ancient writings tell us that it is a 'wise man who leaves an inheritance for his or her children's children.' That is great logically, but we have to realize that if we do not know anything about money or how it works, then how will we translate that into the information necessary for our children and their children to benefit from our knowledge?

Stated differently, if you do not get a clear understanding of how money works, by study and by experience, then you will not be able to do the right things with it. The late, great Dr. Myles Munroe taught us that "where the purpose of a thing is unknown, abuse is inevitable." If you do not know the purpose of money, you will abuse it. As a matter of fact, many of us are living a life right now that is associated with abusing money. Many are underwater on home mortgages, overextended on credit cards and oftentimes living from paycheck to paycheck from week to week. Whether it is as simple as overspending at the grocery store or making investment errors, without a clear understanding you will continue to live a life based on that abuse.

**Katrina:**

*Often, our intentions are honorable, yet still we find ourselves in a tough situation based on a bad decision around money. There was a time when I contracted to purchase an apartment building and a house to use as a home for unwed mothers; both very honorable uses for the money. I wrote a check to the broker for escrow in the amount of $50,000. The challenge was that I hadn't learned the first principle around money, and that is to follow your instincts... that inner voice of your intuition. Even though I did not feel good about the situation, I went through with it anyway. Well, the broker did* not deposit the check. Instead, he cashed the check. Even though I attempted to stop payment on the check, it was too late. He absconded with the money. Although he ended up in jail, I never got back my money. This could have been avoided had I operated within established principles of wealth regarding due diligence. Fortunately, I was surrounded by great coaches—my father being one of them. When I told him what happened, he basically told me to shut up and stop crying about it. I was young and I could easily make the money back. Then he showed me where I had made a mistake in my decision making. He was right!! I did make the money again and I did not make the mistake again; and you do not have to either. You can use our knowledge and experience and begin to understand the principles so clearly that you will never make that mistake. You will understand how money works and how to protect yourself from financial pitfalls.

What are some of the little known things that people with money do that people without money do not? Consider a few of these habits of the wealthy:

- The number one habit of wealthy people is that they give 10 percent of their income to charity. Now we personally believe that 10 percent of all of your increase/money should be paid to a church as a tithe. In fact, our goal is to live on 10 percent of our income and give 90 percent away without changing our lifestyle. Whether it is a church, a charity, a family or some other cause, other wealthy people make sure that they give at least 10 percent back to people in need and organizations that mean something to them.

- Wealthy people know where their money is and whether it was invested or spent. When money is simply spent, it deducts from overall net worth and does not offer the promise of a greater return. When money is invested, it adds to net worth and offers an increase toward the return of investment. Wealthy people do not lose track of their money and they do not spend it frivolously. For example, some would say, it is only a soda costing $2.00. Well multiply that $2.00 x 365 days and it totals $730. What could you do with an extra $730? Exactly. Beware of using the word 'only' when it comes to your money.

- Wealthy people shop around. According to market research on wealth creation, the wealthy do not buy items they desire from the first place that they find what they are looking for. They look for the best bargain. Most wealthy people shop at places like Nordstrom and Target. When they find what they are looking for, they generally negotiate to save even more money. Their mantra is 'everything's negotiable' and they realize that it is not what you make, it is what you keep that counts. They rarely buy on impulse, but use the same cautious approach with shopping as they do with investing.

Remember, faith is a magnet so put your faith out there and expect the unexpected; believe the unbelievable and watch God take what you have and multiply it for generations to come.

## Chapter 6

## *Embrace the Philosophy of Paying it Forward:*
*You are Blessed to be a Blessing*

What does the idea of 'Paying it Forward' mean to you? Whether you're basing this concept on the popular movie with a similar title, or interpreting it from scriptures regarding blessing others, or likening the idea to simply being a good person, the message behind the words is a very positive one. In its simplest terms, paying it forward means to pass along your good fortune to someone else, especially by doing something for them that they couldn't do for themselves. When you are the recipient of a gift or blessing, the expectation is that you, in turn, will be a blessing to someone else and they in turn will be a blessing to someone else and so on and so on.

Have you ever been on the receiving end of someone else's kindness or generosity? Automatically, you probably experienced feelings of relief and gratitude—and maybe even a desire to pass along that feeling to someone else. It's amazing how the simplest act of kindness or compassion can generate so much goodness. In our opinion, those feelings come from the realization that we aren't necessarily deserving of other people's kindness, so when someone goes out of their way to be nice, we are even more sensitive to what it means. In the same way, those same feelings are generated from being the gift giver too. There's something special about helping someone who is in need. It fulfills an inherent inner purpose that we all have to contribute to a cause greater than our own. Giving fulfills our innate need to feel needed and as though we have contributed to our world in a positive way. For some, the sense of gratification is balanced with the fact that they are blessed with enough resources to share, which is definitely something to be thankful for.

'Blessed to be a blessing' is practically a cliché now, but what does it actually mean? To be blessed is to demonstrate ability to receive and appropriately utilize resources. Blessings may come in the form of health, wealth and surroundings. To be a blessing means that we are able to serve as a conduit and redirect resources to a place where they can accomplish the most good. Essentially, when we use the phrase 'blessed to be a blessing,' we're saying that we have more than enough good things in our lives that we can share with others who may be experiencing lack in a particular area.

Years ago, there was a division within congregations and denominations about whether Christians were supposed to be materially blessed or not. In one camp were people who insisted that poverty was next to godliness, and focus on anything other than the Word of God was approaching heresy and blasphemy. In the other camp were people who insisted that God was and is concerned about the totality of our lives, including material things that have more earthly value than eternal value. Although there are still differing opinions about the topic, it appears that both sides of the argument have come a little closer to the middle and decided to meet halfway. If we were to summarize the compromise it would sound something like this: As children of God, we are blessed to be a blessing. It is okay for us to have things, as long as the things don't have us. For example, it is not sinful or ungodly to work for a large corporation and carry a high-ranking title, as long as that title does not define who you are and embolden you to misuse or abuse your power and mistreat others. Another example would be that it is okay to have a nice home, as long as the home does not become an idol of false worship and a haven used to exclude other people who may not share in your good fortune.

We would argue that being blessed is a requirement in a faith-filled life because it is the result of God's promise to bless His children. Being blessed is a prerequisite to building up the necessary reserves to assist others in a time of need. If you've ever been on a flight and paid attention to the safety instructions, one of the things you've heard is: 'In the case of an emergency, oxygen masks will drop down from the overhead panel. Please secure your own mask before attempting to assist others.' Even the Bible, in the book of Luke, tells the physician to 'heal thyself' – to do the good work they've admired in other places in their own land. In other words, you can't help anyone else until you first help yourself.

How can you feed the hungry if you are also broke and starving? How will you be able to send deserving young students to college or help keep someone in their home if you're living paycheck to paycheck and barely making ends meet? It's no coincidence that the scriptures teach more about money and wealth than they do about heaven and hell. The Bible is our guide for the here and now, not the hereafter. It is right now, in this earthly existence, that we are called to serve and bless others. We cannot be naïve about the realization that our society is built on the foundation of capitalism and it is money that makes this world go round. The Bible even foretold the importance of money and material wealth by stating in Ecclesiastes 10:19, that 'money answers all things; or that money can be an answer to anything.' Now, to be clear, money is not always the right answer for every set of circumstances, but in many situations, money opens the door to solutions that resolve problems.

Think about it... money may not result in divine healing, but it can provide better health insurance and medical care. For parents with a sick child, more money for better treatment to take care of their child is just what the doctor ordered. Money may not mend broken family relationships, but it can underwrite the game plan for a better education and a new start in life. Money doesn't make people smart or wise, but it does give them access to better educational opportunities. So even if money isn't the right answer, money is usually linked to an answer to solve a problem.

In the Body of Christ, 'reaping what we sow' is a common theme. Yes, it is true that you will reap *what* you sow, but you are not always going to reap *where* you sowed it. Many people look at the person they just blessed and expect them to be a blessing right back. Instead, just focus on being a blessing in every single opportunity and in every single environment, realizing that your harvest can come from any direction. Why put limits on where your blessings come from? World renowned salesman and motivational speaker Zig Ziglar said, "what you make happen for others ultimately, God will make happen for you." Keep sowing into the lives of others, because you definitely will reap the rewards.

People who have an understanding or appreciation of farming and agriculture seem to grasp the concept of 'sowing and reaping' very well, because that's what the idea is based upon. Seeds are the life-source implantations that are sown into the ground, and the harvest is what develops and grows from the seed to produce the end product. In life, there are literal seeds and there are theoretical seeds. Sometimes we plant a physical object with the expectation of a physical result. Other times we plant an idea or sentiment with the expectation of something similar in return. It's not at all uncommon to hear a person say, "Well, you reap what you sow." Basically, they are telling someone that they got the result of what they planted into a situation. Want to know what to expect in your life? You need not look any further than the types of seeds you've been planting.

Some people seem to attract favor, blessings and good things into their lives." In most cases, they are simply reaping the harvest from the seeds they have spent a lifetime sowing. It's hard to be kind and good to people without kindness and goodness coming back in return. On the other hand, some people seem to consistently attract trouble, hardship and strife. Again, most likely, they are simply collecting the results of what they have sown into the world. Our words and actions carry energy, which can be positive or negative. When we generate positive energy, we also attract positive energy. When we generate negative energy, we also attract negative energy. Aren't you drawn to people who laugh, smile and make you feel comfortable and at ease? The goodwill they exude makes them more attractive to people, who in kind, return the favor. However, think about what is sown and reaped when someone is rude or unkind. The immediate reaction to rudeness is more rudeness and unkindness, which reaps an undesirable harvest.

The other side of the equation is that this interaction is not just about the seeds, it's also about the soil. We cannot plant good seeds into poor soil and expect a bountiful harvest. As spiritual farmers, we are called to be good stewards of the resources that God gives us. When we throw away or waste our seeds, we will not reap the expected results. We've all been there. Almost everyone can remember doing someone a favor, or going out of your way to help someone else, expecting some sort of gratitude in return. Instead of gratitude, there is silence—or worse, there is an expectation or sense of entitlement and taking for granted our generosity. Nothing irritates people like having someone demonstrate a lack of gratitude. (God probably thinks the same thing about us). The mistake is if we keep planting good seeds into the same poor soil, hoping that the soil will change. There are things that farmers do to improve soil quality, but those remedies are not always immediate. We can use fertilizer, manure, new soil and water, but the results take time. A better use of our resources is to do a careful examination of the soil and to be more careful where we plant our valuable seeds.

What results when good seeds meet good soil is a bountiful harvest. The seeds are in a good environment that actually nurtures their potential to grow. The farmer is attentive and consistent in caring for the seeds by ensuring that they receive plenty of water and sunshine, and by removing weeds that could possibly disrupt or choke the plant. The soil serves as a good home that fosters development of the seed, and nothing external is allowed to hinder the process. In that ideal scenario, the combination of good seeds and good soil creates an optimal environment for success. That is the same combination that we are aspiring toward in life. When we take care to invest our seeds into good opportunities that offer a significant return, we experience the spiritual and natural benefits of sowing and reaping.

When we consider the parameters of sowing and reaping, we are encouraged to think beyond our own existence. The Bible often speaks of being a blessing to our "children's children." In theory and in practice, God wants us to plan and support the work of four generations. We are to honor our parents, provide for our families, support our children and prepare for our grandchildren. Surely, that is no easy task. But if that's what God is instructing us to do, then there also must be an expectation that He will provide the resources we need in order for us to accomplish such a tall order. The work we do, and the seeds we sow, are not just for us and our immediate gratification. We are to think in terms of how we can break generational curses and how we can inspire generational blessings.

> *Honor your parents, provide for your family, support your children and prepare for your grandchildren.*

In any family, simple observation will identify patterns of behavior that are noticeable and predictable over a series of decades. In some families, the issue might be vices that include alcoholism or substance abuse. In other families, the issue might be related to broken marriages and broken homes. Regardless of what the problems are, the reality is that the same problems keep popping up over and over again. Sowing and reaping has a lot to do with that. On the other hand, there are families whose lineage is a reflection of peace and harmony and financial prosperity. It seems like almost everything they touch turns to gold. The same process and principle of sowing and reaping is in effect, and similar patterns of belief and behavior throughout the familial links and generations will be evident.

Pay it forward and you will truly be blessed to be a blessing. We have the responsibility to do that, because if we have our blessings and things that we have been afforded, and we sit on those things and we do not help others around us, then our communities as a whole begin to suffer. If our communities suffer, then our states will suffer; then our country, and ultimately our world. We have a natural and spiritual duty, as we are learning and progressing, to pay it forward by empowering ourselves and empowering others who are around us—and paving the way for those who will come after us.

# Chapter 7

# Multiple Streams of Income for Kingdom Purposes:
## Expand Your Territory

Sometimes, your financial situation is such that you simply need more money. Our philosophy, which may be a little different than yours, is that rather than talking about cutting expenses in order to meet financial obligations, we should talk about ways to increase income. This is not to the exclusion of making sure you are not overspending and/or wasting money. This is in addition to those areas. However, as we learned in the very first chapter of this book, what you focus on, you attract. Focusing on decrease and lack will get you more decrease and lack. In the same way, focusing on increase and advancement will get you more increase and advancement.

What we really believe and what we are trying to help people with, is really thinking through additional ways in which they could possibly earn income. The truth is that during times of uncertainty, it can be scary out there. If the supervisor on your job comes and says, "we've got to cut back," what do you do? You need to have an answer to these questions:

- Do we have some things in place that will protect us in the next few months while we get things together?

- Have we set things up for the worst case scenario?

- Do we have something else that will prop up the table of our lives if one of the legs falls off—or if it becomes unstable?

The time is now to begin working on a plan that diversifies your incoming revenue options and expands your financial territory.

Having multiple streams of income is a biblical principle. When you have set a standard for yourself, in terms of who you are, what you are going to deal with, and what you are going to put up with, you will begin to make different decisions. In a job situation like Katrina was in, it frustrated her that as a mother, she had to ask the employer for time off to spend with a sick child or attend a school event. Having multiple streams of income in place ensures that when something at work does not align with your priorities, with what's important to you, there are other options available.

At the Thousandaire Academy, we look at different mechanisms to make multiple streams of income possible so that you "don't end up with all your eggs in one basket." Do not have all of your money coming from one source, because that strategy is too risky. If that source dries up, where does that leave you and your family? Obviously, your options for additional income include traditional business, network marketing and even using your own expertise to turn your passion into profit. There are many different ways that you can go out there and make some things happen, you will want to figure those things out in advance. Some of you who are reading this book already have other businesses and/or streams of income. Whether you do or not, we must talk about increasing your income... making more money. Here are a few examples of opportunities to diversify your revenue sources.

**Network Marketing.** We are strong proponents of network marketing for many reasons. Typically, there is a low cost of entry, a small investment to participate in a system that someone else has already built the infrastructure and consequently made the large investments; yet you can build to whatever income level you choose. Regardless of your background—whether you are a doctor, a lawyer or a painter; whether you have an education or not—you start at the same place as everyone else with the same opportunity and the only thing you need to win is a burning desire! In any network marketing opportunity, you are the only variable. You all have the same product or service and the same compensation plan. YOU are the only variable. If anyone in the company has had success, you can have it too. As with anything in the Thousandaire Academy, we will help you follow through with the due diligence necessary to make sure your investment is a sound one. Network marketing companies legally leverage the power of volume, in purchasing and sales—allowing you to grow your business by increasing the number of contacts and connections you make to deliver goods and services.

Are you recommending that we take part in a 'pyramid scheme?' Of course, we are not. Things to avoid in this process would include pyramid schemes that are built based on using funds from one source to cover another, laundering money among friends and family members. Pyramid structures in business have only become nefarious based on the few unscrupulous people who base their entire business on recruiting new members and their payments versus the sale of reputable products and services in networking marketing or direct sales. It is important to know the difference, before you invest.

**Traditional Business.** Even still, others are more attracted to traditional business opportunities, like a brick and mortar or home-based company. Part of the process with the Thousandaire Academy is helping you to find your personal expertise, and package it in such a way that you can monetize it. Believe it or not, some of what you have experienced is marketable. How many years have you been on that job? What did you go through to get there? Are you a great parent? Do you know how to cook? There are some things that you do and have done—that you have tons of experience in—that people would not only love to know how to do, they would pay money for someone to teach them. You will leave the Thousandaire Academy module clear about how to package You Inc., in a way that you can create additional income.

More than any other time in history, now is the best time to use your own knowledge, life experiences, and career expertise to start a business. The internet has leveled the playing field by allowing you to reach the entire connected planet to provide your specific solution. Believe it or not, people are willing to pay you for helping them shorten their learning curve or by providing them with the step by step process to achieving what you have achieved in your life. More than that, if you are able to provide people with ways to avoid or overcome obstacles, you could be well on your way to discovering a new income opportunity for yourself. In the Thousandaire Academy, Jai shares his 5-point framework for taking your knowledge and experiences and creating a business that pays.

**Investing.** We will begin to deal with both beginning and advanced strategies in terms of investing. Everybody wants to make money in the stock market, real estate and other areas, yet no one really knows where to go to get the information. Even though it is everywhere, we have brought it all together in one convenient place you, with expert testimonies, insights and experiences.

## REVENUE IDEAS

| Revenue Source | Initial Investment | Weekly Time Commitment | Monthly Revenue Generated | Current Financial Return | Annual Financial Goal |
|---|---|---|---|---|---|
| | | | | | |
| Ex. Subscriber-based blog | $19.99/month ~$240/year | 5 hours per week | $1,000 per month | $12,000 per year | $25,000 per year |
| | | | | | |
| | | | | | |
| | | | | | |
| | | | | | |
| | | | | | |
| | | | | | |

# Chapter 8

## Thousandaire Academy:
### Bringing it all Together

Why Thousandaire Academy? Because talent alone is not enough. Your success will also require additional skills, training, networking and perseverance to build the legacy you want to leave. In the Academy, we help you to bring it all together.

There is an organization called The Institute, which helps small businesses grow into bigger businesses. Although their primary focus is on supporting business professionals in the southeastern and mid-Atlantic regions of the country, their impact is nationwide. Recently, The Institute published a blog titled, "Talent is Not Enough." With their permission, we want to share it with you:

**Talent is Not Enough**. There's a great saying in military training that, "Hard work beats talent when talent is not working hard enough." If that's true, it's no wonder that so many talented individuals are still struggling to get ahead and to make their business idea a success. Truth be told, there are millions of talented people still hoping and wishing for their dreams to come true. While there are some folks with basic skills and average ability who get up every day and hustle—learning the necessary skills, getting the necessary training, and putting in the necessary effort—to make positive things happen. And like it or not, they are often the ones who get what they want out of life, because they've already figured out that talent alone is not enough. They realized (sooner rather than later) that achieving their goals not only requires talent, but also skill, passion, dedication, drive, and perseverance.

Whether it's sports, business, entertainment, or something else, those who are recognized as the greatest masters of their craft all have something in common. They dedicate themselves 100 percent to becoming the best at what they do. They combine raw talent with work—and a plan for success. They don't look for or accept shortcuts, and they don't make excuses when things don't go their way. Champions don't blame the rules, they don't blame the competition or their circumstances; they accept responsibility and they learn, grow, and adapt as needed. They take ownership of their success and their shortcomings, and use every opportunity as a springboard forward toward their ultimate goal. If you're planning to launch your idea or grow your organization, keep these thoughts in mind:

**Play to your strengths.** If you're a sprinter, don't focus on running marathons. Jamaican sprinter Usain Bolt is known as one of the most successful track stars because he spends his time and energy doing what he does well. If Bolt started to compete in marathons, he most likely would lose. Why? Because he is a natural-born sprinter. As a result, he spends his time training and competing in sprints...not marathons. Sure, an occasional marathon here or there might help his endurance, but it will not sustain his career. Early-on, Bolt and his coaches/trainers identified his strengths and used that information to implement a successful game plan. Successful people do what they do best, and they do it repeatedly. They don't get sidetracked with inconsequential activities that distract them from their goals and priorities. In other words, 'they keep the main thing, the main thing.'

**Delegate and focus.** You can't be and don't need to be all things to all people. It's really difficult to be the visionary CEO of your company if you're also the CFO, personnel manager, intern, receptionist, and janitorial staff. Learn to direct your time, energy, and attention toward the tasks you do well and delegate the other duties to someone who can perform them better and more efficiently than you. In the game of business, lack of focus is one of the most common reasons for the lack of success.

**Surround yourself with people smarter than you.** Some people's world is so small, they're the biggest thing in it. Do an assessment of your professional circle and surroundings. If you're the smartest and most successful person in your group, it's time to expand your network and broaden your circle of influence. It's true that "water seeks its own level." While it's important to have trusted colleagues, friends, and confidantes, it's also important not to become complacent with individuals who only tell you what you want to hear. True leaders and visionaries are surrounded by talented individuals who can and do challenge their thinking and ideas—forcing them to expand their perspective. Attending networking events for new and different industries is a good way to meet new people, embrace new ideas, and combine talent with the resources needed to accomplish your goals. (Copyright 2016 - TheInstituteNC.org and @TheInstituteNC)

Now that you have read this entire book, we want to be sure that you have been able to apply some—if not all—of the principles to your life. While your life can change based on these principles, if you are serious about accelerating your life and increasing your finances, you are going to want to join us in the Thousandaire Academy. The principles discussed in this book are explored in more depth in our comprehensive Thousandaire Academy program. Whether you are physically located at home on your computer, on your cell phone or somewhere else, you can access your coursework in the Thousandaire Academy. When you become a student, you will have a personal log-in so that you can move systematically through the training. The course software actually keeps track of your progress and communicates with your coaches as to how you are progressing. This allows us to help you stay on course. You set the pace for completing the information and exercises that will change your life.

There are 7 complete modules of the Thousandaire Academy, titled the same as the chapters in this book. Each module has videos, affirmations, worksheets and action items. They are constantly being updated and our students have the opportunity to review them at their leisure. What you will not be able to do, however, is jump around the modules. They are systematically laid out and their order must be followed.

Additionally, in the Academy, there are extra bonuses that are important for you to have more success in a shorter timeframe.

**Accountability.** You will become part of a private and exclusive Facebook group that includes other students of the Thousandaire Academy. There you will be able to exchange ideas, ask questions and perhaps most importantly, give (and receive) praise to other people when they have made a good financial decision and encourage them when they make a mistake. As a team we can proclaim, "I stuck to my plan, because I am in it to win it." There is nothing like having that kind of accountability and support. It is our concept of peer pressure and positive associations. This way, everyone around you is moving in the same direction; a team that has got your back, your front and both sides. A tribe that will encourage you when you need encouragement, and kick your butt when your butt needs kicking.

**Live Events.** Additionally, we host a live event (at least one) each year. You can attend with your spouse or another guest and literally connect in person with some of the experts you have read about, watched their videos or even talked with on a 1-on-1 basis.

**Experts.** Our relationships over the years have yielded us great access to some amazing people. We did the research and found them for you. We brought them in, interviewed them, asked them the probing questions that we know that you want to ask and get answered, and we've got all of it sitting there waiting for you. How this system will work is with video. It is with checklists and PDFs that you fill out and follow along. It is really amazing how we've done it and tailored it to fit your lifestyle. We have not only the video, but we also have audio, so you can listen and learn while on the go.

Yes, there are other programs or plans available out there that cost more money and deliver less opportunity for engagement around your specific situation. They just do not give you the content. They do not give you the access. They do not give you the plan or the road map. We are going to give you what you need to go ahead do it yourself or, should you mutually decide, you can connect with some of the experts and take part in their programs for additional assistance.

As we have been building this syllabus, we have done an assessment and gotten feedback on our layout and information. Our mentors and other industry experts, even our students, are wondering how we are doing so much for such a small investment. With all of the experts and details, their expectation is that this class would cost a lot of money. We have been advised to charge in excess of $5,000 for this training. If a program is going to teach you what you need to know in this way, it is well worth it. However, we are also following our own advice by investing in you and sowing into quality soil. We have designed this program to be a part of our lifelong legacy as a result of our mandate to build the Kingdom.

Someone is probably saying, "I am considering the Thousandaire Academy because of my money challenges. Why should I pay anything at all?" That is easy. Because free has no value. If it were free, you wouldn't take it seriously. You wouldn't make the changes. You wouldn't do the work. You wouldn't be responsive to the instruction and you'd be wasting everybody's time. Yours, ours—it just wouldn't make any sense. We are serious about solving financial problems, because if it makes "sense" for you now, it will make dollars for you later. If it makes dollars for you later, you are going to look up and be in the Thousandaire Club. Once you are in the Thousandaire Club, it is just a couple more steps to the Millionaire Club. So, no, we are not going to do it for free. Besides, *price is only an issue in the absence of value and it is value that you are really after, isn't it?*

Are you ready to get started? Right here and now, we want you to make the decision to improve your life and begin taking steps toward your future financial security. Whichever way you go, whether it is $1,000 in full or you choose to make 3 payments of $350 to get started in the Academy, just do it. We are waiting to see you on the other side, because once you log in and get signed up, we are going to be right there waving at you, helping you create the strategy to change your story. We look forward to welcoming you into the Academy, to hearing your story, to seeing and meeting you; but more than that, to hearing your success stories about how the Thousandaire Academy is changing what you do, so that you can have what you want in your life. Remember **First Thousands Then Millions**.

**Visit us online to learn more:**

www.ProjectThousandaire.com

www.ThousandaireAcademy.com

| Professional Speaker | Radio Personality |
| Successful Entrepreneur | Inspirational Leader |
| Professional Networker | Author & Publisher |
| Life Coach/Trainer | Chaplain/Minister |

***Katrina Ferguson*** delivers a passionate, enthusiastic and entertaining message to both teach and encourage you to celebrate your individuality and breakthrough to become your 'greater self.' Her inspiring message is based upon lessons learned in her own breakthrough journeys. Ms. Ferguson is committed to helping others across the world apply these principles in their individual lives and relationships. In her unique, uncompromising style, she brings life changing principles and leadership skills to inspire and motivate thousands across age, gender and industry lines. Featured in national publications, including *Essence* Magazine and *USA Today*, Ms. Ferguson has been the subject of numerous articles and interviews and her story is currently being used all over the country to train and motivate sales forces of both public and private organizations. She routinely shares the stage with company presidents and executives as she conducts trainings and presentations around the country and has spoken for several faith-based organizations including the Potter's House in Dallas, Texas and Evangel Cathedral in Upper Marlboro, Maryland.

Ms. Ferguson speaks from her experience and success in the traditional corporate fields of real estate, financial services and law, as well as her success as an entrepreneur having owned and operated several successful businesses, including a publishing company (publisher of the Amazon Best Selling books, *Footnotes: a 31-Day Leadership Guide for Women* and *The Queens' Legacy),* retail establishments and a personal fitness studio. Her acute understanding and ability to inspire people has enabled her to excel in the network marketing industry. Her keen awareness that conflicting demands, resource constraints and shifting priorities are challenges that must be overcome for success in today's global marketplace has placed her in constant demand as a presenter, motivator, and trainer of trainers by sales organizations across the nation. Ms. Ferguson regularly conducts conference calls and training events for publicly traded companies, privately held corporations, entrepreneurs and faith-based organizations.

Ms. Ferguson encourages everyone to be passionate and uncompromising in 'giving back' to the community and celebrating their ability do so. She has served as Chaplain for the WNBA Washington Mystics team, a member of the Board of Directors for the Women In Business Network of America (WIBNA) and the Founder and President of *A Sister's Love*, a nonprofit organization, whose mission is to provide practical information, tangible and intangible tools to assist women and children in achieving while propelling them into greatness. She has raised thousands of dollars for faith-based organizations and has invested thousands of hours performing community service.

Utilizing customized presentations, a powerful stage presence, insightful delivery and fresh insight, Ms. Ferguson will entertain, train and inspire your audience to new levels of enthusiasm and achievement. For more information, to purchase Ms. Ferguson's materials or to request an appearance, please contact The Ferguson Group by calling 703-906-1711, e-mailing Katrina@KatrinaFerguson.com or visiting www.KatrinaFerguson.com.

***Jai A. Darden*** is a business/marketing consultant, personal mastery coach, speaker, author, and a *Champion* for those with a dream. As a successful business leader, he has led and advised organizations with up to $2 billion in total assets. He helps both domestic and international businesses transform and fortify their strategy by increasing their ROI while maintaining the integrity of their mission. Jai is a welcomed and trusted advisor to many CEOs and executives and frequents the boardrooms of some of the most successful and influential companies in the country.

Based on his success as a business and marketing consultant, best-selling authors, subject matter experts and businesses of varied sizes and niches trust Jai's guidance in growing their businesses.

As a speaker, his words are captivating and provoking. He challenges audiences to think and to walk away not only inspired but informed and moved to action. These unique attributes have led him from speaking at local business forums, to Bar Associations, to addressing business and church groups ranging in the tens of thousands of people. His message of *Bold* faith, servitude and triumph bolsters empowerment to those who listen and receive it.

Before striking out on his own to follow his passion for helping people and businesses alike to achieve success, he worked his way through the ranks in corporate America. Jai quickly became recognized as a high producing and performing manager. His performance produced quick business performance turnarounds, years of consecutive year-over-year double-digit business growth, and loyal customer bases.

More importantly, Jai was revered as a people developer and was respected for fostering cultures of success. He received numerous awards and honors. For example, as a Vice President with JP Morgan Chase Bank, N.A. Jai received the prestigious National Top Manager Award twice and was interviewed by the JP Morgan Chase News Source Publication (reserved for the Top 5 percent P&L performing managers).

One day, a client of the bank walked into Jai's office and challenged him by saying that he could impact more people and businesses on his own. Jai took this to heart, as he was already having an internal struggle about launching his consulting business. He left the cozy corner office and took the leap of faith.

Jai has taken all that he has learned throughout his decorated career in the corporate world, and has leveraged it into a business that is impacting people and organizations. Jai has a passion for those who are looking to tap into their God-given talents. He is often quoted as saying, *"You have everything you need within you to become your best self. You were perfectly and beautifully made. Now, go claim what is already yours."* Through his personal mastery coaching programs, he helps individuals see their potential and encourages them to act on it to achieve goals and dreams that would be otherwise left to die.

He faithfully serves as the Executive Pastor at his local church assembly where his father is the Founder and Senior Pastor of the 40-year-old ministry. Jai is the CEO and Lead Project Consultant for New Day Success Strategies, a business consultancy and personal mastery coaching firm. He resides in Houston, TX with his loving wife, where they are devoted parents to their two young boys. For more information, please contact New Day Success Strategies at (888) 391-1008 or email adrienne@newdayss.com.

# IT'S YOUR TIME

EDUCATION | TRAINING | MENTORING

www.ThousandaireAcademy.com
ACADEMY@PROJECTTHOUSANDAIRE.COM

---

1·844·343·9829

**Katrina Ferguson
& Jai A. Darden**
*Your Coaches*

Over the next 12 months, 1,000 individuals and families will be positioned to make solid, educated decisions to earn, save and grow thousands, which can ultimately turn into millions as we assist churches and their members in being faithful with the little so it ultimately becomes much. (Luke 16:10).

Utilizing a fun, engaging and results-based system, Project Thousandaire will move you and your congregation
**First Thousands
Then Millions.**

**15-Minute Free Financial Consultation**

**Financial Education Conference for Your Local Church**

**Financial & Personal Development**

www.ProjectThousandaire.com

www.ingramcontent.com/pod-product-compliance
Lightning Source LLC
Chambersburg PA
CBHW050650160426
43194CB00010B/1883